JAN   1998

noted
8-11-13
back page
ripped

Orland Park Public Library
14921 Ravinia Avenue
Orland Park, IL 60462
708-428-5100

DEMCO

Jack and Jill's
Adventure
in Alphabet Town

by *Janet Riehecky*
illustrated by *Linda Hohag*

created by Wing Park Publishers

CHILDRENS PRESS ®
CHICAGO

Library of Congress Cataloging-in-Publication Data

Riehecky, Janet, 1953-
    Jack and Jill's adventure in Alphabet Town / by Janet Riehecky ;
illustrated by Linda Hohag.
        p.   cm. — (Read around Alphabet Town)
    Summary: Jack and Jill meet several "j" words on their
adventure in Alphabet Town. Includes alphabet activities.
    ISBN 0-516-05410-4
    [1. Alphabet—Fiction.]   I. Hohag, Linda, ill.   II. Title.
III. Series.
PZ7.R4277Jac   1992
[E]—dc 20   91-20541
                                                         CIP
                                                         AC

Jack and Jill's
Adventure
in Alphabet Town

You are now entering Alphabet Town,
With houses from "A" to "Z."
We're going on a "J" adventure today.
Come, see what fun it will be.

This is the "J" house of Alphabet
Town. Jack and Jill live here.
Their house is on a hill.

Jack and Jill like "j" things.

They like to

jump rope.

And they like to work

jigsaw puzzles.

But most of all, they like to ride their

jeep

down the hill. "Jolly good fun,"
says Jill.

Sometimes friends visit Jack and Jill.
They play

jacks.

They climb on the

jungle gym

and ride in Jack and Jill's jeep.

One day Jack and Jill invited
their friends to a show.

First, they served jelly sandwiches and juice.

15

Then it was time for the show to begin.

Jill went first. Her jewelry
jingled as she danced a jig.

Then Jack did some

judo.

First he jumped high in the air.
Then he jabbed with his feet...

and landed with a jolt. "Jimminy
Cricket," he said.

Next Jack and Jill told jokes.
Jill asked, "Jack, why are you
jumping up and down?"

And Jack answered, "I just took some medicine. The bottle said, 'Shake before using,' but I forgot to jiggle it."

The next act was Jack and his jumping beans. The beans jumped from a

jar into a jack-o-lantern.

And last, Jill juggled jellybeans.

"Oh, no," she said. "The jumping beans are jumbled in with the jelly beans."

Jill jumped after the jumping beans.
"Just my luck," she said. "I have
spoiled the show."

Then Jill tumbled off the stage and down the hill. Jack tried to help Jill, but he went tumbling after her.

All their friends joined in. In a jiffy, everyone was in a jumble at the bottom of the hill.

"That was lots of fun," everyone
said. "You put on a good show.
Let us do one for you tomorrow."

"Jolly good idea!" said Jill.
"Now let's jog back up the hill."

And off they jogged up the hill
to the ''J'' house of Jack and Jill.

MORE FUN WITH JACK AND JILL

What's in a Name?

In our "j" adventure, you read many "j" words. Our names begin with "J." Many of our friends' names begin with "J" too. Here are a few.

Janet

Jean

Jonathan

Jared

Jacob

Jane

Do you know other names that start with "J"?
Does your name start with "J"?

Jack and Jill's Word Hunt

We like to hunt for "j" words. Can you help us find the words that begin with "j" on this page? How many are there? Can you read the words?

jet

jacket

flapjacks

jeans

turtle

pajamas

Can you find any words with "J" in the middle? Can you find a word with no "J"?

31

Jack and Jill's Favorite Things

"J" is our favorite letter. We love "j" things. Can you guess why? You can find some of our favorite "j" things in our house on page 7. How many "j" things can you find there? Can you think of more "j" things?

Now you make up a "J" adventure.